Ellyn Sanna

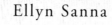

EVERYDAY
Grace

*Spiritual Refreshment
for Women*

BARBOUR
PUBLISHING

© 2011 by Barbour Publishing, Inc.

ISBN 978-1-61626-218-1

Contents

Introduction

Grace is a gift we did nothing to earn. When we were kids, grace was finding out there was a snow day when we thought we would have to go to school. Today, in our adult lives, grace comes to us in many shapes and forms. It is birdsong and the sun on our faces on a day when nothing else seems to go right; a child's hand in ours; a friend's understanding smile. And most of all, grace is the gift of God's unconditional love. Grace is Jesus, the One who saves us and heals us and never stops loving us. Some days we get so busy that we forget to see the gifts of grace that fill our lives. But God's grace is always there, waiting to be noticed, waiting to be enjoyed.

Achievement

Ever Wider

A longing fulfilled is a tree of life.
PROVERBS 13:12 NIV

Take stock of your life. What were you most hoping to achieve a year ago? (Or five years ago?) How many of those goals have been achieved? Sometimes, once we've reached a goal, we move on too quickly to the next one, never allowing ourselves to find the grace God wants to reveal within that achievement. With each goal reached, His grace spreads out into your life, like a tree whose branches grow ever wider.

A Solid Foundation

*A bad motive can't achieve
a good end.*

PROVERBS 17:20 MSG

We hear it all the time: The end justifies the means. But that is not how it works in the kingdom of God. It's like trying to build a beautiful house on a shaky foundation. It just doesn't work. Sooner or later, the weak foundation will affect the rest of the house.

True achievement is built on God's grace and love. That is the kind of foundation that holds solid no matter what.

Perfection

*I don't mean to say that
I have already achieved these
things or that I have already
reached perfection. But I press on
to possess that perfection for which
Christ Jesus first possessed me.*

PHILIPPIANS 3:12 NLT

We are called to be perfect. Nothing else is good enough for God's people. That doesn't mean we have an inflated sense of our own worth. And it doesn't mean we beat ourselves up when we fall short of perfection. We know that in our own strength we can never hope to achieve perfection—but with God's grace, anything is possible.

Balance

Steady. . .

*People with their minds set on you,
you keep completely whole,
steady on their feet, because they
keep at it and don't quit.*

Isaiah 26:3 MSG

One of the meanings of *grace* is "an effortless beauty of movement." A person with this kind of grace doesn't trip over her own feet; she's not clumsy or awkward, but instead she moves easily, fluidly, steadily. From a spiritual perspective, most of us stumble quite a bit—and yet we don't give up. We know that God holds our hands, and He will keep us steady even when we would otherwise fall flat on our faces.

Christ-Balance

*Jesus caught them off balance
with his own test question:
"What do you think about the Christ?
Whose son is he?"*

MATTHEW 22:41 MSG

Sometimes Christ asks us to find new ways
of thinking. . .new ways of living. . .new ways
of encountering Him in the world around
us. That is not always easy. We don't like
to be caught off balance. When our life's
equilibrium is shaken, we feel anxious, out
of control. But if we rely on Christ, He will
pick us up, dust us off, and give us the grace
to find our balance in Him.

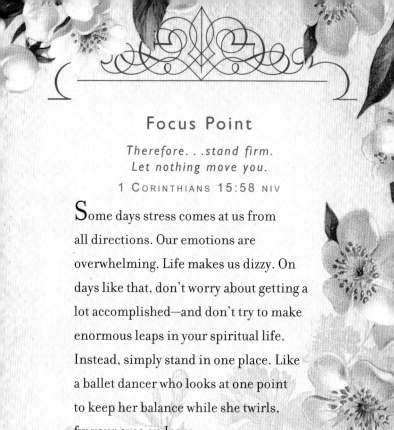

Focus Point

Therefore. . .stand firm.
Let nothing move you.

1 CORINTHIANS 15:58 NIV

Some days stress comes at us from
all directions. Our emotions are
overwhelming. Life makes us dizzy. On
days like that, don't worry about getting a
lot accomplished—and don't try to make
enormous leaps in your spiritual life.
Instead, simply stand in one place. Like
a ballet dancer who looks at one point
to keep her balance while she twirls,
fix your eyes on Jesus.

Grounded
in Love

*"You'll be built solid,
grounded in righteousness,
far from any trouble—
nothing to fear!"*

Isaiah 54:12 MSG

Balance isn't something we can achieve
in ourselves. Just when we think we have
it all together, life has a tendency to come
crashing down around our ears. But
even in the midst of life's most chaotic
moments, God gives us grace; He keeps
us balanced in His love. Like a building
that is built to sway in an earthquake without
falling down, we will stay standing if we
remain grounded in His love.

Integrity

*People with integrity walk safely,
but those who follow crooked
paths will slip and fall.*

PROVERBS 10:9 NLT

Achieving balance in life is seldom
easy. We're likely to go too far in first one
direction and then another. But despite our
tendency to wobble, God's grace leads us
always forward. He keeps us from staggering
too far off the path. As we follow Him,
choosing a path of integrity rather than one
of selfishness and lies, we will find our
way easier, our footing surer, and our
balance steadier.

Beauty

True Beauty

What matters is not your outer appearance—the styling of your hair, the jewelry you wear, the cut of your clothes—but your inner disposition. Cultivate inner beauty, the gentle, gracious kind that God delights in.

1 Peter 3:3–4 MSG

We want to be beautiful. It's a longing that has been in our hearts since we were little girls. As grown-up women, we can become overly worried about our appearance, fretting over whether we measure up to the demanding standards of that little girl who still lives in our hearts. We need to relax in the assurance of God's grace within us. As we allow His Spirit to shine through us, we will find our deepest, truest beauty.

Bible

New Insight

*Your word is a lamp to guide my feet
and a light for my path.*

PSALM 119:105 NLT

We sometimes take the Scriptures for
granted. These ancient words, though,
continue to shine with light just as they did
centuries ago. In them, God's grace is
revealed to us. In them, we gain new
insight into ourselves and our lives.

Deepest Truths

*For the word of God
is alive and powerful.
It is sharper than the sharpest two-
edged sword, cutting between soul
and spirit, between joint and marrow.
It exposes our innermost
thoughts and desires.*

HEBREWS 4:12 NLT

God's words are not merely letters on a page. They are living things that work their way into our hearts and minds, revealing the fears and hopes we've kept hidden away, sometimes even from ourselves. Like a doctor's scalpel that cuts in order to heal, God's Word slices through our carefully created facades and exposes our deepest truths.

For Generations

*I inherited your book on living;
it's mine forever—what a gift!
And how happy it makes me!*

PSALM 119:111 MSG

Think of it! God's Word is ours. We can hear His voice in scripture—and apply it to our own lives. Generation upon generation has followed this amazing book of life, and now it is our turn. In the Bible, each and every day, we find God's grace revealed.

Blessings

Just What We Need

God can pour on the blessings in astonishing ways so that you're ready for anything and everything, more than just ready to do what needs to be done.

2 CORINTHIANS 9:8 MSG

Blessings are God's grace visible to us in tangible form. Sometimes they are so small we nearly overlook them—the sun on our faces, the smile of a friend, or food on the table—but other times they amaze us. Day by day, God's grace makes us ready for whatever comes our way. He gives us exactly what we need.

Life and Nourishment

*"I, the Lord, am the one who answers
your prayers and watches over you.
I am like a green pine tree;
your blessings come from me."*

HOSEA 14:8 NCV

Think of it: God is like a tree growing at
the center of your life! In the shade of this
tree, you find shelter. This tree is ever
green, with deep roots that draw up life and
nourishment. Each one of life's daily
blessings is the fruit of this tree. It is
the source of all your life, all your joy,
and all your being.

Blessing Others

"Bless those who curse you.
Pray for those who hurt you."

LUKE 6:28 NLT

Not only does God bless us, but we are
called to bless others. God wants to show
the world His grace through us. He can
do this when we show our commitment to
make God's love real in the world around
us through our words and actions, as
well as through our prayer life. We offer
blessings to others when we greet a
scowl with a smile, when we refuse to
respond to angry words, and when we offer
understanding to those who are angry and
hurt.

Walk Confidently

*"But blessed are those who trust
in the Lord and have made the Lord
their hope and confidence."*

JEREMIAH 17:7 NLT

What gives you confidence? Is it your clothes. . .your money. . .your skills? These are all good things, but they are blessings from God, given to you through His grace. When your hopes (in other words, your expectations for the future) rest only in God, then you can walk confidently, knowing He will never disappoint you.

Children

A Gift

*Don't you see that children
are God's best gift?*

PSALM 127:3 MSG

Whether we have children of our own or enjoy others' children, God's grace is revealed to us in a special way through these small people. In children, we catch a glimpse of what God intended for us all, before we grew up and let life cloud our hearts. Children's hope gives us grown-ups hope as well. Their laughter makes us smile, and their love reminds us that we, too, are loved by God.

Peace

*"I will teach all your children,
and they will enjoy great peace."*

ISAIAH 54:13 NLT

It's hard not to worry about the children in our lives. Many dangers threaten them, and our world is so uncertain. We can do our best to teach and guide the children we love, but in the end we must trust them to God's grace, knowing that they must find their own relationship with Him— and that as they know Him, they will find peace, even in the midst of the world's uncertainty.

A Special Kind of Grace

Oh, how blessed are you parents,
with your quivers full of children!
Your enemies don't stand a chance
against you; you'll sweep them right
off your doorstep.

PSALM 127:4–5 MSG

What are your worst enemies? Despair?

Self-doubt? Selfishness? We all face

enemies like these. But God's grace comes

to us in a special way through children.

As we love them, we find hope; we focus

outward and forget about ourselves. And

somehow those funny little people manage

to sweep our enemies right off the doorsteps

of our hearts!

Small Things

"The greatest among you must become like the youngest."

In some ways, we need to look to children as our role models. We get so used to functioning in the adult world, loaded down with responsibilities, that we forget the child's knack for living in the present moment, for taking delight in small things, for loving unconditionally. Jesus asks us to let go of our grown-up dignity and allow ourselves to enter into His presence as children. When we do, we encounter His grace anew.

25

Absolute Certainty

From everlasting to everlasting
the LORD's love is with those who
fear him, and his righteousness
with their children's children.

PSALM 103:17 NIV

We can rely on God's love not only for ourselves but also for the children in our lives, those little people we love, whose lives we touch. As we send those children out into the world so terribly vulnerable, we can know with absolute certainty that God's grace goes with them. Just as God's love reached us through our parents and the other adults who shaped our lives, God will also spread His love to the generations to come.

Creation

Look Up!

*The heavens declare the glory
of God; the skies proclaim the
work of his hands.*

PSALM 19:1 NIV

Grace is as near as the sky over your
head. Look up and be reminded of how
wonderful God truly is. The same God
who created the sun and the atmosphere,
the stars and the galaxies, the same God
who day by day creates a new sunrise
and a new sunset, that same God loves
you and creates beauty in your life
each day!

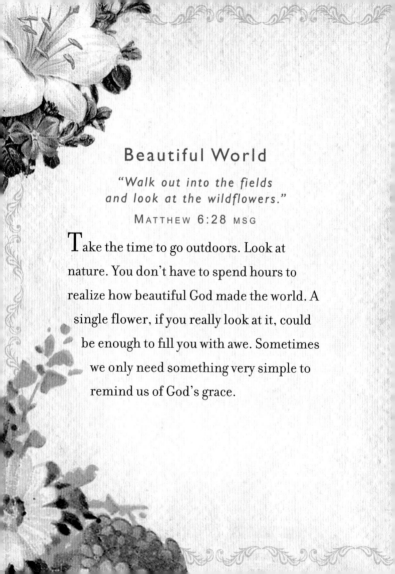

Beautiful World

*"Walk out into the fields
and look at the wildflowers."*

MATTHEW 6:28 MSG

Take the time to go outdoors. Look at nature. You don't have to spend hours to realize how beautiful God made the world. A single flower, if you really look at it, could be enough to fill you with awe. Sometimes we only need something very simple to remind us of God's grace.

Direction

Law of Love

*I pondered the direction of my life,
and I turned to follow your laws.*

PSALM 119:59 NLT

Did you know that the word *law* comes
from root words that mean "foundation" or
"something firm and fixed"? Sometimes we
can't help but feel confused and uncertain.
When that happens, turn to God's law,
His rule for living. Love is His law, the
foundation that always holds firm. When
we cling to that, we find direction.

Sound Advice

*Without good direction, people lose
their way; the more wise counsel you
follow, the better your chances.*

PROVERBS 11:14 MSG

Often God makes use of other people when
He wants to guide you. His grace flows to you
through others' experiences and wisdom.
Keep your ears open for His voice speaking
to you through the good advice of those you
trust.

Grace for Each Day

May the Lord direct your hearts into God's love and Christ's perseverance.

2 THESSALONIANS 3:5 NIV

Allow God to lead you each day. His grace will lead you deeper and deeper into the love of God—a love that heals your wounds and works through you to touch those around you. Just as Christ never gave up but let love lead Him all the way to the cross, so, too, God will direct you all the way, giving you the strength and the courage you need to face each challenge.

Closer to Him

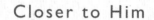

*"When the Spirit of truth
comes, he will guide you
into all truth. He will not speak
on his own but will tell you
what he has heard."*

JOHN 16:13 NLT

God's Spirit is truth. In Him there are no lies. You can trust Him absolutely to lead you ever closer to God. This is how you recognize true grace: It will always bring you nearer to the One who loves you most, the God who created you and gave Himself for you. If you find yourself somewhere else, you have not been following the Spirit.

Discipline

Leading

*But since we belong to the day,
let us be self-controlled, putting on
faith and love as a breastplate, and
the hope of salvation as a helmet.*

1 THESSALONIANS 5:8 NIV

We sometimes think of discipline as a negative thing, as something that asks us to sacrifice and punish ourselves. But really the word has more to do with the grace we receive from instruction and learning, from following a master. Like an athlete who follows her coach's leading, we are called to follow our Master, wearing His uniform of love and His helmet of hope.

Follow Jesus

*"Whoever serves me must follow me;
and where I am, my servant
also will be. My Father will honor
the one who serves me."*

JOHN 12:26 NIV

A disciple is someone who follows.
That is the discipline we practice: We
follow Jesus. Wherever He is, we go. In His
presence we find the daily grace we need
to live. As we serve Him, God honors us;
He affirms our dignity and makes us all we
were meant to be.

Christlike

Don't sin by letting anger control you.
Think about it overnight
and remain silent.

Psalm 4:4 NLT

A disciple must practice certain skills until she becomes good at them. As Christ's disciples, we are called to live like Him. The challenge of that calling is often hardest in life's small, daily frustrations, especially with the people we love the most. But as we practice saying no to anger, controlling it rather than allowing it to control us, God's grace helps us develop new skills, even ones we never thought possible!

Life's Circumstances

My child, do not reject the
LORD's discipline, and don't get
angry when he corrects you.
The LORD corrects those he loves,
just as parents correct the child
they delight in.

PROVERBS 3:11–12 NCV

God doesn't send us to time-out, and He
certainly doesn't take us over His knee and
spank us. Instead, His discipline comes to
us through the circumstances of life. By
saying yes to whatever we face, no matter
how difficult and frustrating it may be,
we allow God's grace to infuse each moment
of our day. We may be surprised to find
that even in life's most discouraging
moments, God's love was
waiting all along.

Encouragement

Reach Out to Him

"Your words have supported those who were falling; you encouraged those with shaky knees."

JOB 4:4 NLT

God knows how weak and shaky we feel some days. He understands our feelings. After all, He made us, so He understands how prone humans are to discouragement. He doesn't blame us for being human, but He never leaves us helpless, either. His grace is always there, like a hand held out to us, simply waiting for us to reach out and grasp it.

Reach Out to Others

Whoever has the gift of encouraging others should encourage.

ROMANS 12:8 NCV

Just as God encourages us, He wants us to encourage others. The word *encourage* comes from Latin words that mean "to put heart or inner strength into someone." When God encourages us, His own heart reaches out to us and His strength becomes ours. As we rely on His grace, we are empowered to turn and reach out to those around us, lending them our hearts and strength.

Reciprocal

When we get together, I want to
encourage you in your faith, but I also
want to be encouraged by yours.

Romans 1:12 NLT

Encouragement is always reciprocal.
When we encourage others, we are
ourselves encouraged. In the world's
economy, we pay a price in order to
receive something we want; in other
words, we give up something to get
something. But in God's economy, we
always get back what we give up. We are
connected to each other, like parts of
a body. Whatever good things we do
for another are good for us as well.

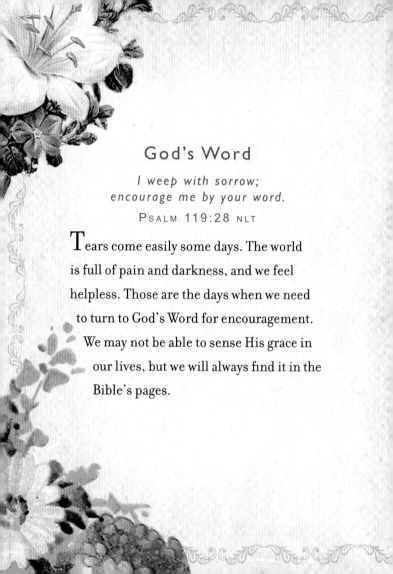

God's Word

I weep with sorrow;
encourage me by your word.

PSALM 119:28 NLT

Tears come easily some days. The world is full of pain and darkness, and we feel helpless. Those are the days when we need to turn to God's Word for encouragement. We may not be able to sense His grace in our lives, but we will always find it in the Bible's pages.

Faith

By His Grace

A person is made right with God through faith, not through obeying the law.

ROMANS 3:28 NCV

Human laws can never make us into the people we are meant to be. No matter how scrupulous we try to be, we will always fall short. Our hands and hearts will come up empty. But as we fix our eyes on God, committing our lives and ourselves to Him, we are made right. We are healed and made whole by His grace, exactly as God meant us to be.

Heartfelt

For we live by believing
and not by seeing.

2 CORINTHIANS 5:7 NLT

The world of science tells us that only what can be seen and measured is truly real. But our hearts know differently. Every day, we depend on the things we believe—our faith in God and in our friends and family, our commitment to give ourselves to God and others—and it is these invisible beliefs that give us grace to live.

Unfailing Love

But I trust in your unfailing love.
I will rejoice because you
have rescued me.

Psalm 13:5 nlt

Have you ever done that exercise in trust where you fall backward into another person's arms? It's hard to let yourself drop, trusting that the other person will catch you. The decision to let yourself fall is not an emotion that sweeps over you. It's just something you have to do, despite your fear. In the same way, we commit ourselves to God's unfailing love, finding new joy each time His arms keep us from falling.

Safe in Christ

*This is what God commands:
that we believe in his Son,
Jesus Christ, and that we love each
other, just as he commanded.*

1 JOHN 3:23 NCV

Again and again, the Bible links faith and
love. Our human tendency is to put up walls
of selfishness around ourselves, to protect
ourselves at all costs. God asks us instead
to believe daily that we are safe in Christ
and to allow ourselves to be vulnerable
as we reach out in love to those around us.

Family

Sticking Together

Families stick together in all kinds of trouble.

PROVERBS 17:17 MSG

Families can drive you crazy. Whether it's the people with whom you share a house, or the extended family that gets together at holidays and birthdays, family members can be exasperating, even infuriating. When it comes right down to it, though, your family members are the ones who show you God's grace even when life is hard, the ones who stick by you no matter what (even when they make you crazy!).

"Extended" Family

God sets the lonely in families.

PSALM 68:6 NIV

God knows that we need others. We need
their love and support, their understanding,
and their simple physical presence nearby.
That is why He gives us families. Families
don't need to be related by blood, though.
They might be the people you work with,
or the people you go to church with, or the
group of friends you've known since grade
school. Whoever they are, they're the people
who make God's grace real to you every day.

Family Ties

Jesus, who makes people holy,
and those who are made holy
are from the same family.
So he is not ashamed to call them
his brothers and sisters.

HEBREWS 2:11 NCV

You and Jesus are family! Jesus, the One who made you whole and clean in God's sight, is your Brother. Family ties connect you to Him and to all those with whom He is connected. In Christ, we find new connections with each other. By His grace, we are now kinfolk.

No Division

*In Christ's family there can
be no division into Jew and
non-Jew, slave and free,
male and female.
Among us you are all equal.*

GALATIANS 3:28 MSG

Grace is a gift that none of us deserve—and
by grace Jesus has removed all barriers
between God and ourselves. God asks that as
members of His family we also knock down
all the walls we've built between ourselves
and others. Not just the obvious ones,
but also the ones that may hide in our
blind spots. In Christ, there is no liberal or
conservative, no educated or uneducated, no
division whatsoever.

Feelings

Sensitivity

*At the same time, don't be callous
in your exercise of freedom, thoughtlessly
stepping on the toes of those who aren't
as free as you are. I try my best to be
considerate of everyone's feelings in all
these matters; I hope you will be, too.*

1 Corinthians 10:32–33 MSG

The person who walks in grace doesn't trip
over other people's feet. She doesn't shove
her way through life like a bull in a china
shop. Instead, she allows the grace she has
so freely received to make her more aware
of others' feelings. With God-given
empathy, she is sensitive to those
around her, sharing the grace she
has received with all she meets.

Back to God

My dear brothers and sisters, always be willing to listen and slow to speak. Do not become angry easily, because anger will not help you live the right kind of life God wants.

JAMES 1:19–20 NCV

Our feelings are gifts from God, and we should never be ashamed of them. Instead, we need to offer them all back to God, both our joys and our frustrations. When we give God our anger, our irritation, our hurt feelings, and our frustrations, we make room in our hearts to truly hear what others are saying.

Perception

"The Lord himself goes before you and will be with you; he will never leave you nor forsake you. Do not be afraid; do not be discouraged."

DEUTERONOMY 31:8 NIV

The world we see with our eyes is only a piece of reality, a glimpse into an enormous and mysterious universe. Just as our eyes often deceive us, so do our feelings. We perceive life through our emotions, but they are as limited as our physical vision. Whether we sense God's presence or not, He is always with us. Grace waits to meet us in the future, so we can disregard all our feelings of fear and discouragement.

Letting Go

A peaceful heart leads to
a healthy body; jealousy is
like cancer in the bones.

PROVERBS 14:30 NLT

Some emotions are meant to be
nourished, and others need to be quickly
dropped into God's hands. Learn to
cultivate and seek out that which brings
peace to your heart. And practice letting
go of your negative feelings as quickly
as you can, releasing them to God. If
you cling to these dark feelings, they
will reproduce like a cancer, blocking the
healthy flow of grace into your life.

Food

True Nourishment

He gives food to every living thing.
His faithful love endures forever.

PSALM 136:25 NLT

People often have a confused relationship with food. We love to eat, but we feel
guilty when we do. We sometimes turn to
food when we're tense or worried, trying
to fill the empty, anxious holes in our
hearts. But God wants to give us the true
nourishment we need, body and soul,
if only we will let Him.

53

Healthy

" 'Give us today our daily bread.' "
MATTHEW 6:11 NIV

We need food each day. Healthy fruits and vegetables, whole grains, lean protein for our bodies—and times of prayer and quiet for our souls. Like a loving mother, God delights in nourishing His children.

Daily Miracles

"That is why I tell you not to worry about everyday life—whether you have enough food and drink, or enough clothes to wear. Isn't life more than food, and your body more than clothing?"

MATTHEW 6:25 NLT

With our eyes fixed on what we *don't* have, we often overlook the grace we have already received. God has blessed us in many ways. Our bodies function day after day in amazing ways we take for granted, and life is filled with an abundance of daily miracles. Why do we worry so much about the details when we live in such a vast sea of daily grace?

Hungry

*You serve me a six-course
dinner right in front of my enemies.
You revive my drooping head;
my cup brims with blessing.*

PSALM 23:5 MSG

At the end of a long day, do you ever feel
weak and ravenous with hunger? You've
gone too long without eating, and now your
body demands food! We often do the same
thing to our spirits, depriving them of
the spiritual nourishment they need—
and then we wonder why life seems so
overwhelming and bleak. But dinner is
on the table, and God is waiting to revive
us with platefuls of grace and cups
brimming with blessings.

Forgiveness

God's Honor

For the honor of your name, O LORD, forgive my many, many sins.

PSALM 25:11 NLT

Like all gifts of grace, forgiveness by its very definition is nothing that can ever be earned. Forgiveness is what God gives us when we deserve nothing but anger. He forgives us not because we merit it, but because of His own honor. Over and over, we will turn away from God—but over and over, He will bring us back. That is who He is!

Wholly and Completely

*"Forgive others, and you
will be forgiven."*

Luke 6:37 NLT

The words *forgive* and *pardon* come
from very old words that mean "to give
up completely and wholeheartedly."
When we forgive others, we totally give up
our rights to feel we've been injured or
slighted. And in return, God's grace totally
fills the gaps left behind when we let go of
our own selfishness. As we give ourselves
wholeheartedly to others, God gives Himself
completely to us.

Reasonable?

"If you see your friend going wrong, correct him. If he responds, forgive him. Even if it's personal against you and repeated seven times through the day, and seven times he says, 'I'm sorry, I won't do it again,' forgive him."

LUKE 17:3–4 MSG

As humans, we tend to feel that forgiveness has reasonable limits. A person who repeats the same offense over and over can't be very serious when he or she asks for forgiveness!

It makes sense from a human perspective. But fortunately for us, God isn't reasonable. He forgives our sins no matter how many times we repeat them. And He asks us to do the same for others.

Lavish and Abundant

*Let them come back to God,
who is merciful, come back to our God,
who is lavish with forgiveness.*

ISAIAH 55:7 MSG

God's forgiveness is never stingy or grudging. And He never waits to offer it to us. Instead, it's always there, a lavish, abundant flood of grace, just waiting for us to turn away from our sin and accept it.

Friends

Unconditional Grace

A friend loves at all times.

PROVERBS 17:17 NASB

Friends are the people you can allow to see you at your worst. They're the ones who can see you without your makeup. . .or walk in when your house is a mess. . .or overhear you acting like a thirteen-year-old—and they'll still be your friends. They reveal to you God's unconditional grace.

Our Companion

*Our LORD, you are the friend
of your worshipers, and you make
an agreement with all of us.*

PSALM 25:14 CEV

God is our Friend. He is our companion through life's journey; He is the One who always understands us; and no matter what we do, He always accepts us and loves us. What better agreement could we ever have with anyone than what we have with God?

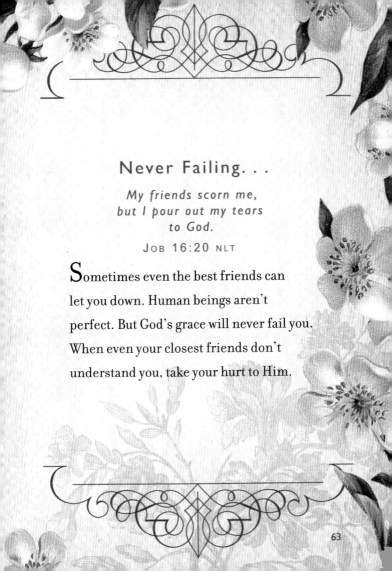

Never Failing. . .

My friends scorn me,
but I pour out my tears
to God.

JOB 16:20 NLT

Sometimes even the best friends can
let you down. Human beings aren't
perfect. But God's grace will never fail you.
When even your closest friends don't
understand you, take your hurt to Him.

Taking Turns

Two people are better off
than one, for they can help each
other succeed. If one person falls,
the other can reach out and help.
But someone who falls alone
is in real trouble.

ECCLESIASTES 4:9–10 NLT

Have you ever noticed that in the best
friendships, you take turns being needy?
You're strong enough to help your friend
one day—and the next day, she's the one
offering you comfort and help. Over and
over, God uses our friends to make His
grace real in our lives. And He wants
to use us to spread His grace back to our
friends.

Fulfillment

What You Crave

*Take delight in the Lord, and he will
give you your heart's desires.*

PSALM 37:4 NLT

Do you ever feel as though God wants to
deny you what you want, as though He's
a cruel stepparent who takes pleasure in
thwarting you? That image of God is a
lie. He's the One who placed your heart's
desires deep inside you. As you turn to Him,
knowing that He alone is the source of all
true delight, He will grant you what
your heart most truly craves.

Satisfied

Satisfy us in the morning with your un-
failing love, that we may sing for
joy and be glad all our days.

PSALM 90:14 NIV

God wants to fulfill you. He wants you to
feel satisfied with life so that you will catch
yourself humming or singing His praises
all day long. Even when life is hard, He is
waiting to comfort you with His unfailing
love so that gladness will creep over your
heart once more.

The Next Oasis

The LORD will always guide you and provide good things to eat when you are in the desert. He will make you healthy. You will be like a garden that has plenty of water or like a stream that never runs dry.

ISAIAH 58:11 CEV

God wants you to be healthy—not just physically, but emotionally, intellectually, and spiritually as well. He wants to fill your life full of all the things you truly need. The life He wants for you is not dry and empty and barren. Instead, it is lush and full of delicious things to nourish you. We all have to cross life's deserts sometimes, but even then God will supply what you need to reach the next oasis He has waiting.

Expressions
of Grace

*So I decided there is nothing
better than to enjoy food and drink
and to find satisfaction in work.
Then I realized that these pleasures
are from the hand of God.*

ECCLESIASTES 2:24 NLT

Hedonists are people who have decided
that life's only meaning lies in physical
pleasures. But they can't escape God's
hand. Our food, our drink, the
satisfaction we take in our work, and all
the physical pleasures of our lives are
not separate from God. Instead, they are
expressions of His grace. He longs for us
to be fulfilled in every way possible.

Future

Wonderful Plans

"For I know the plans I have for you,"
says the LORD. "They are plans for good
and not for disaster, to give
you a future and a hope."

JEREMIAH 29:11 NLT

Don't worry about the future. No matter
how frightening it may look to you sometimes, God is waiting there for you. He has
plans for you, wonderful plans that will lead
you deeper and deeper into His grace
and love.

Safe

My life is in your hands.
Save me from my enemies and
from those who are chasing me.

PSALM 31:15 NCV

Do you ever feel like trouble is chasing you? No matter how fast you run or how you try to hide, it comes relentlessly after you, dogging your footsteps, breathing its hot breath down your neck, robbing you of peace. What's even worse is that it waits for you down the road as well!

Maybe you need to stop running and hiding and instead let yourself drop into God's hands, knowing He will hold your future safe.

Wonderful Things

Everything God made is waiting with excitement for God to show his children's glory completely.

ROMANS 8:19 NCV

Some days it's hard to feel very optimistic. We listen to the evening news and hear story after story about natural disasters and human greed. God doesn't want us to be ostriches, hiding our heads in the sand, refusing to acknowledge what's going on in the world. But He also wants us to believe that the future is full of wonderful things He has planned. The whole world is holding its breath, waiting for God's wonderful grace to reveal itself.

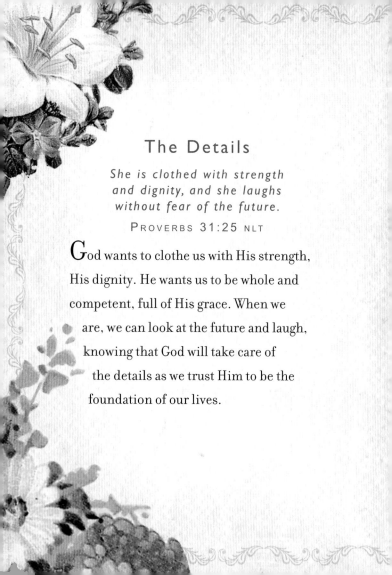

The Details

*She is clothed with strength
and dignity, and she laughs
without fear of the future.*

PROVERBS 31:25 NLT

God wants to clothe us with His strength,
His dignity. He wants us to be whole and
competent, full of His grace. When we
are, we can look at the future and laugh,
knowing that God will take care of
the details as we trust Him to be the
foundation of our lives.

Happiness

Happiness Requirement. . .

*I'm just as happy with little as with much,
with much as with little. . . .
Whatever I have, wherever I am, I can
make it through anything in the One
who makes me who I am.*

PHILIPPIANS 4:12 MSG

When you were younger, what did you think you needed to be happy? Nice clothes? A boyfriend? A husband? A good job? At the point where you are in your life now, what is it you think your happiness requires? Day after day, God blesses us, but our happiness does not depend on those blessings. Our joy depends only on God. When we realize that, we no longer have to worry about losing or gaining life's blessings.

Simply Happy

Are any of you happy?
You should sing praises.

JAMES 5:13 NLT

Some days are simply happy days. The sun shines, people make us laugh, and life seems good. A day like that is a special grace. Thank God for it. As you hum through your day, don't forget to sing His praises
.

Good for You!

A happy heart is like good medicine, but a broken spirit drains your strength.

PROVERBS 17:22 NCV

God longs to make you happy. He knows that happiness is good for you. Mentally and physically, you function better when you are happy. Discouragement and sadness sap your strength. It's like trying to work while carrying a heavy load on your back: It slows you down and makes everything harder.

Let God heal the breaks in your spirit. His grace can make you strong and happy.

Rescued!

*The LORD wants to show
his mercy to you. He wants to
rise and comfort you. The LORD is
a fair God, and everyone who waits
for his help will be happy.*

ISAIAH 30:18 NCV

God doesn't want you to feel lonely and
unhappy. He waits to bring you close to
Him, to comfort you, to forgive you.
Wait for Him to rescue you from life's
unhappiness. His grace will never let
you down. Keep your eyes fixed on Him,
and you will find happiness again.

Health

For Eternity

My health may fail, and my spirit
may grow weak, but God remains
the strength of my heart;
he is mine forever.

PSALM 73:26 NLT

Sooner or later, our bodies let us down.
Even the healthiest of us will one day have to
face old age. When our bodies' strength fails
us, we may feel discouraged and depressed.
But even then we can find joy and strength
in our God. When our hearts belong to the
Creator of the universe, we realize we are far
more than our bodies. Because of God's
unfailing grace, we will be truly
healthy for all eternity.

The Entire Package

He makes the whole body fit together perfectly. As each part does its own special work, it helps the other parts grow, so that the whole body is healthy and growing and full of love.

EPHESIANS 4:16 NLT

God has a holistic perspective on health. He sees your body, soul, heart, and mind, and He wants each part of you to be strong and fit. He looks at our world in the same way, longing to heal the entire package— society, the environment, and governments. He wants His body on earth, the church, to be whole and strong as well. Health pours out of Him, a daily stream of grace on which we can rely for each aspect of life.

Choosing Cheerful

*A cheerful disposition is good
for your health; gloom and
doom leave you bone-tired.*

PROVERBS 17:22 MSG

Have you ever heard the saying "You may not be able to keep birds from perching on your head, but you can keep them from building nests in your hair"? It means we can't always control our emotions, but we *can* choose which ones we want to hold on to and dwell on. Choosing to be cheerful instead of gloomy is far healthier for our minds, bodies, and spirits. Being depressed is exhausting!

Whole and Healthy

When Jesus heard this,
he told them, "Healthy people
don't need a doctor—sick people do.
I have come to call not those who
think they are righteous, but those
who know they are sinners."

MARK 2:17 NLT

With Jesus, we never need to pretend to be something we aren't. We don't need to impress Him with our spiritual maturity and mental acuity. Instead, we can come to Him honestly, with all our neediness, admitting just how weak we are. When we do, we let down the barriers that keep Him out of our hearts. We allow His grace to make us whole and healthy.

Holy Spirit

Free!

*For the Lord is the Spirit,
and wherever the Spirit of the
Lord is, there is freedom.*

2 CORINTHIANS 3:17 NLT

How do you know when the Holy Spirit is present in your life? You should be able to tell by the sense of freedom you feel. If you feel oppressed, obsessed, or depressed, something in your life is out of kilter. Seek out God's Spirit. He wants you to be free.

Breathing

In certain ways we are weak, but the Spirit is here to help us. For example, when we don't know what to pray for, the Spirit prays for us in ways that cannot be put into words.

ROMANS 8:26 CEV

The Holy Spirit is the wind that blows through our world, breathing grace and life into everything that exists. He will breathe through you as well as you open yourself to Him. We need not worry about our own weakness or mistakes, for the Spirit will make up for them. His creative power will pray through us, work through us, and love through us.

His Instrument

"The Spirit of the Lord is on me, because he has anointed me to preach good news to the poor. He has sent me to proclaim freedom for the prisoners and recovery of sight for the blind, to release the oppressed."

LUKE 4:18 NIV

Just as the Holy Spirit wants you to be free, He also wants to use you as His instrument to breathe freedom and hope into the world. Be His instrument today. Tell people the truly good news that God loves them. Do whatever you can to spread freedom and vision and hope. Be a vehicle of the Spirit's grace.

Spirit-Oxygen

Tell me this one thing:
How did you receive the Holy Spirit?
Did you receive the Spirit by
following the law? No, you received
the Spirit because you heard the
Good News and believed it.

GALATIANS 3:2 NCV

As we share the good news of Christ, we need to take care that we are not preaching the law rather than the love of Christ. The Spirit did not come into your heart through legalism and laws—and He won't reach others through you if that is your focus. Breathe deeply of grace, and let it spread from you to a world that is desperate for the oxygen of the Spirit.

Home

A Lovely Place

How lovely is your dwelling place,
O Lord Almighty!

Psalm 84:1 NIV

Imagine this: God considers your heart His home! It's the place where He dwells. And as a result, your heart is a lovely place, filled with the grace of the almighty God.

A Special Place

My people will live in peaceful
places and in safe homes and
in calm places of rest.

ISAIAH 32:18 NCV

Home is the place where you feel most comfortable—the place where you can kick off your shoes, put on your bathrobe, and relax. God has created this place for you, a place where His grace can soothe your heart in a special way.

Longing for Home

*This is what the LORD says: "You will
be in Babylon for seventy years.
But then I will come and do for you all
the good things I have promised,
and I will bring you home again."*

JEREMIAH 29:10 NLT

Sometimes in life we go through periods when we feel out of place, as though we just don't belong. Our hearts feel restless and lonely. We long to go home, but we don't know how.

God uses those times to teach us special things we need to know. But He never leaves us in exile. His grace always brings us home.

Filled with Grace

*"There is plenty of room for
you in my Father's home.
If that weren't so, would I have
told you that I'm on my way to
get a room ready for you?"*

JOHN 14:2 MSG

None of us knows exactly what lies on the
other side of death's dark door. But we do
know this: death will take us home. Jesus
promised us that. He wouldn't have said
it just to make us feel better; Jesus wasn't
one for telling polite lies! So we can trust
that right now He is getting our home
in heaven ready for us, filling it with grace.
When we enter the door, we will find it is
exactly right for us, the place for which
we have always longed.

Hope

Unchanged

Why am I discouraged?
Why is my heart so sad?
I will put my hope in God!

PSALM 42:5 NLT

Thousands of years ago, the psalmist who wrote these words expressed the same feelings we all have. Some days we just feel blue. The world looks dark, everything seems to be going wrong, and our hearts are sad. Those feelings are part of the human condition. Like the psalmist, we need to remind ourselves that God is unchanged by cloudy skies and gloomy hearts. His grace is always the same, as bright and hopeful as ever.

Amazing Expectations

*Listen to my voice in the morning, L*ORD*.*
Each morning I bring my requests
to you and wait expectantly.

PSALM 5:3 NLT

You need to get in the habit of hoping. Instead of getting up in the morning and sighing as you face another dreary day, practice saying hello to God as soon as you wake up. Listen for what He wants to say to your heart. Expect Him to do amazing things each day.

An Attitude

*God proves to be good to the
man who passionately waits,
to the woman who diligently seeks.
It's a good thing to quietly hope,
quietly hope for help from God.*

LAMENTATIONS 3:25 MSG

Hope is an attitude, not an emotion. It means putting our whole hearts into relying on God. It means keeping our eyes focused on Him no matter what, waiting for Him to reveal Himself in our lives. God never disappoints those who passionately wait for His help, who diligently seek His grace.

Hospitality

Grace of Hospitality

*When God's people are in need,
be ready to help them. Always
be eager to practice hospitality.*

ROMANS 12:13 NLT

God opens Himself to you, offering you
everything He has, and He calls you to do
the same for others. Just as He made
you welcome, make others welcome
in your life. Don't reach out to others
grudgingly, with a sense of obligation.
Instead, be eager for opportunities to
practice the grace of hospitality.

Open Homes

Be quick to give a meal to the hungry, a bed to the homeless—cheerfully.

1 Peter 4:9 msg

Because our homes are our private places, the places we retreat to when we're tired to find new strength, it's hard sometimes to open our homes to others. It's bad enough that we have to cope with others' needs all day long, we feel, without having to bring them home with us! But God calls us to offer our hospitality, and He will give us the grace to do it joyfully.

Grace in Return

*"Then those 'sheep' are going to say,
'Master, what are you talking about?
When did we ever see you hungry and
feed you, thirsty and give you a
drink? . . .' Then the King will say,
'I'm telling the solemn truth: Whenever
you did one of these things to someone
overlooked or ignored, that was
me—you did it to me.'"*

MATTHEW 25:37–40 MSG

If Christ were sitting on our doorstep,
lonely and tired and hungry, what would
we do? We like to think we would throw
the door wide open and welcome Him into
our home. But the truth is we're given the
opportunity to offer our hospitality to Jesus
each time we're faced with a person in need.
His grace reaches out to us through those
who feel misunderstood and overlooked,
and He wants us to offer that same grace
back in return.

Everyone

If your enemy is hungry, feed him.
If he is thirsty, give him a drink.

PROVERBS 25:21 NCV

It's easy to have our friends over for dinner. Offering our hospitality to the people who give us pleasure is not much of a hardship. But hospitality gets harder when we offer it to the people who hurt our feelings, the people we really don't like very much.

But God calls us to reach out in practical, tangible ways to *everyone*. Seek His grace to do this in some way every day.

Intelligence

Thinking Habits

*And now, dear brothers
and sisters, one final thing.
Fix your thoughts on what is true,
and honorable, and right, and pure,
and lovely, and admirable.
Think about things that are
excellent and worthy of praise.*

PHILIPPIANS 4:8 NLT

Our brains are gifts from God, intended to serve us well, special gifts of grace we often take for granted. In return, we need to offer our minds back to God. Practice thinking positive thoughts. Focus on what is true rather than on lies; pay attention to beautiful things and stop staring at the ugly things in life. Discipline your minds to take on God's habits of thinking.

Beyond
Intelligence

The fastest runner does not always win the race, the strongest soldier does not always win the battle, the wisest does not always have food, . . . Time and chance happen to everyone.

ECCLESIASTES 9:11 NCV

How smart do you think you are? Do you assume you will be able to think your way through life's problems? Many of us do—but God reminds us that some things are beyond the scope of our intelligence. Some days life simply doesn't make sense. But even then, grace is there with us in the chaos. When we can find no rational answers to life's dilemmas, we have no choice but to rely absolutely on God.

All of You

" 'Love the Lord God with
all your passion and prayer
and intelligence and energy.' "

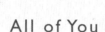

MARK 12:30 MSG

God wants all of you. He wants the
"spiritual parts," but He also wants your
emotions, your physical energy, and your
brain's intelligence. Offer them all to God
as expressions of your love for Him. Let His
grace use every part of you!

Brand-New Ways

*Intelligent people are always
ready to learn. Their ears
are open for knowledge.*

PROVERBS 18:15 NLT

Whether you did well in school or not,
you probably rely on your intelligence
to get you through life. If you're really
intelligent, though, you will remember
that no matter how many years it has been
since you graduated, you are never done
learning. You need to be open to new
ideas, willing to give up old, stale ways
of thinking. When you are, you will
find God's grace revealed in brand-
new ways.

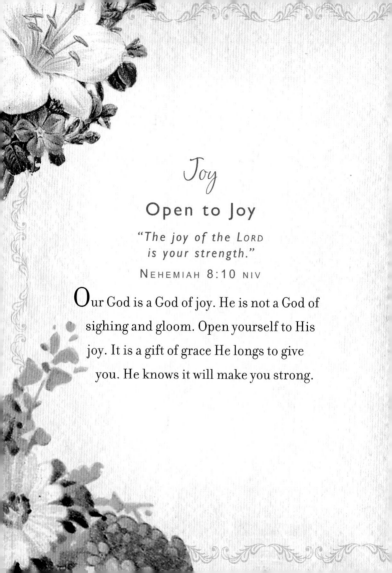

Joy

Open to Joy

*"The joy of the LORD
is your strength."*

Nehemiah 8:10 NIV

Our God is a God of joy. He is not a God of
sighing and gloom. Open yourself to His
joy. It is a gift of grace He longs to give
you. He knows it will make you strong.

Harmony

The hope of the [uncompromisingly] righteous (the upright, in right standing with God) is gladness, but the expectation of the wicked (those who are out of harmony with God) comes to nothing.

PROVERBS 10:28 AMP

When we try to live our lives apart from God, we put ourselves in a place where we can no longer see His grace. Joy comes from being in harmony with God.

Into God's Presence

"He prays to God and finds favor with him, he sees God's face and shouts for joy."

JOB 33:26 NIV

Prayer is the channel through which God's grace flows. We do not pray because God needs us to pray; we pray because *we* need to pray. When we come into God's presence, we are renewed. Our hearts lift. We look into the face of the One who loves us most, and we are filled with joy.

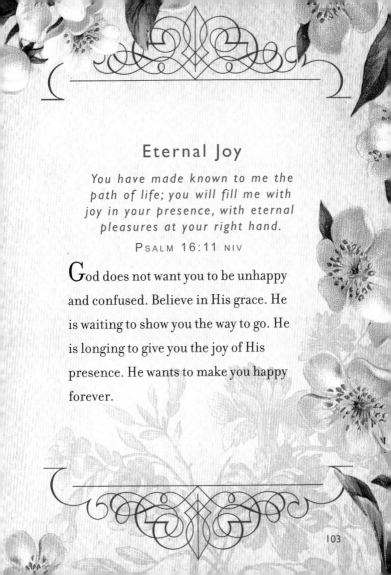

Eternal Joy

You have made known to me the path of life; you will fill me with joy in your presence, with eternal pleasures at your right hand.

PSALM 16:11 NIV

God does not want you to be unhappy and confused. Believe in His grace. He is waiting to show you the way to go. He is longing to give you the joy of His presence. He wants to make you happy forever.

Shine!

*The precepts of the LORD
are right, giving joy to the heart.
The commands of the LORD are
radiant, giving light to the eyes.*

PSALM 19:8 NIV

As children, we probably felt sometimes as though rules had no purpose but to make us miserable. We didn't always understand that our parents' love was behind their rules. As adults, we often have the same attitude toward God's rules. We feel as though a life of sin might be easier, more fun. But instead, it's just the opposite. God always wants what will give us joy. His rules are designed to make us shine.

Kindness

What God Shows Us

*The LORD is righteous in everything
he does; he is filled with kindness.*

PSALM 145:17 NLT

Did you know that the word *kind* comes
from the same root as *kin*? Both words
originally had to do with intimate shared
relationships like the ones that exist
between members of the same family. This
is what God shows us: the kindness of a good
father, the gentleness of a good mother,
the understanding of a brother or
sister.

Rope of Love

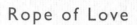

*"I led them with cords of human
kindness, with ropes of love.
I lifted the yoke from their neck
and bent down and fed them."*

HOSEA 11:4 NCV

God's grace is not a lasso looped around
our shoulders, trapping us and binding
us tight. Instead, grace reaches out to us
through the kindness of others. It is a rope
of love that stretches through our lives,
leading us to freedom.

Freely Given

*Out of sheer generosity he put us
in right standing with himself.
A pure gift. He got us out of the
mess we're in and restored us to
where he always wanted us to be.
And he did it by means of
Jesus Christ.*

ROMANS 3:24 MSG

How kind God has been to us! He brought us close to Himself. He reached down and picked us up out of our messy lives. He healed us so we could be the people we were always meant to be. That is what grace is: a gift we never deserved, freely given out of love.

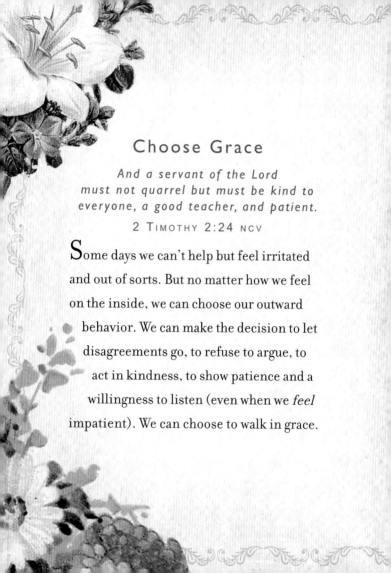

Choose Grace

*And a servant of the Lord
must not quarrel but must be kind to
everyone, a good teacher, and patient.*

2 TIMOTHY 2:24 NCV

Some days we can't help but feel irritated
and out of sorts. But no matter how we feel
on the inside, we can choose our outward
behavior. We can make the decision to let
disagreements go, to refuse to argue, to
act in kindness, to show patience and a
willingness to listen (even when we *feel*
impatient). We can choose to walk in grace.

Laughter

Laugh Out Loud

"He will once again fill your mouth with laughter and your lips with shouts of joy."

JOB 8:21 NLT

Did you know that God wants to make you laugh? He wants to fill you with loud, rowdy joy. Oh, some days His grace will come to you quietly and calmly. But every now and then, you will have days when He makes you laugh out loud.

Transformed

And Sarah declared, "God has brought me laughter. All who hear about this will laugh with me."

GENESIS 21:6 NLT

The first time we read of Sarah laughing, it was because she doubted God. She didn't believe that at her age she would have a baby. But God didn't hold her laughter against her. Instead, He transformed it. He turned her laughter of scorn and doubt into the laughter of fulfillment and grace.

Trust Him

*You people who are now crying
are blessed, because you will
laugh with joy.*

LUKE 6:21 NCV

God's grace comes to you even in the
midst of tears. He is there with you in
your hurt and your sadness. Trust in Him,
knowing that sadness does not last
forever. One day you will laugh again.

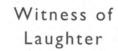

Witness of Laughter

We were filled with laughter, and we sang for joy. And the other nations said, "What amazing things the LORD has done for them."

PSALM 126:2 NLT

Life is truly amazing. Each day, grace touches us in many ways, from the sun on our faces to each person we meet, from the love of our friends and families to the satisfaction of our work. Pay attention. Let people hear you laugh more. Don't hide your joy. It's a witness to God's love.

Life

Full!

"I came that they may have and enjoy life, and have it in abundance (to the full, till it overflows)."

JOHN 10:10 AMP

The life we have in Christ is not restricted or narrow. Grace doesn't flow to us in a meager trickle; it fills our life to the fullest. God's grace comes to us each moment, day after day, year after year, a generous flood that fills every crack and crevice of our lives—and then overflows.

Sing!

*But each day the L*ORD *pours his unfailing love upon me, and through each night I sing his songs, praying to God who gives me life.*

PSALM 42:8 NLT

Life itself is a gift of grace. The very blood that flows through our veins, the beat of our hearts, and the steady hum of our metabolism—all of that is God's free gift to us, a token of His constant and unconditional love. When we are so richly loved, how can we help but sing, even in the darkness?

Surrender

"For whoever wants to save his life will lose it, but whoever loses his life for me will save it."

LUKE 9:24 NIV

Life is full of paradoxes. God seems to delight in turning our ideas inside out and backward. It doesn't seem to make sense, but the only way to possess our life is to surrender it absolutely into God's hands. As we let go of everything, God's grace gives everything back to us, transformed by His love.

Radiant

"If you are filled with light, with no dark corners, then your whole life will be radiant, as though a floodlight were filling you with light."

LUKE 11:36 NLT

We all have dark corners in our lives we keep hidden. We hide them from others. We hide them from God, and we even try to hide them from ourselves. But God wants to shine His light even into our darkest, most private nooks and crannies. He wants us to step out into the floodlight of His love—and then His grace will make us shine.

Love

Love Is Bigger

"Love the LORD your God with all your
heart and with all your soul
and with all your might."

DEUTERONOMY 6:5 NASB

Love is not merely a feeling. It's far bigger
than that. Love fills up our emotions, but it
also fills our thoughts. Our body's strength
and energy feed it. It requires discipline and
determination. Loving God requires the
effort of our whole being.

Act in Love

Let all that you do be done in love.
1 CORINTHIANS 16:14 NRSV

Because love is not merely an emotion, it needs to become real through action. We grow in love as we act in love. Some days the emotion may overwhelm us; other days we may feel nothing at all. But if we express our love while making meals, driving the car, talking to our families, or cleaning the house, God's love will flow through us to the world around us—and we will see His grace at work.

Web of Love

*So now I am giving you a new
commandment: Love each other.
Just as I have loved you,
you should love each other.*

JOHN 13:34 NLT

God's grace comes to us through a
net of relationships and connections.
Because we know we are totally and
unconditionally loved, we can in turn
love others. The connections between
us grow ever wider and stronger, a web
of love that unites us all with God.

Amazing Love

Your unfailing love,
O Lord, is as vast as the heavens;
your faithfulness reaches
beyond the clouds.

Psalm 36:5 nlt

God loves you. The Creator of the
Universe cares about you, and His love
is unconditional and limitless. You can
never make Him tired of you; He will
never abandon you. You are utterly and
completely loved, no matter what,
forever and ever.

Isn't that amazing?

Marriage

Best Clothing

*Above all, clothe yourselves
with love, which binds us all
together in perfect harmony.*

COLOSSIANS 3:14 NLT

Marriage is the place where you are most
vulnerable to another person. Your spouse
is the person who sees you naked, clothed
only in love.

But love is the best clothing. When
as married partners we strip off all our
defensiveness and our selfishness,
nothing comes between us but love.

No Matter What

*Keep your eyes open. . .
give it all you've got, be resolute,
and love without stopping.*

1 CORINTHIANS 16:13 MSG

Married love isn't lace and roses and moonlit nights. That kind of romantic love will come and go throughout a marriage. The kind of love that gets you through dark nights, angry fights, and long, busy days— that love is the resolute kind, the stubborn love that never gives up. That kind of love isn't blind. It needs its eyes wide open so that it can keep on going no matter what.

Money

Thrive!

Whoever trusts in his riches will fall,
but the righteous will thrive
like a green leaf.

PROVERBS 11:28 NIV

Money seems so important in our world. Many things we want depend on money—that remodeling project we're hoping to do, the Christmas gifts we want to give, the vacation we hope to take, and the new car we want to drive. There's nothing wrong with any of those things, but our enjoyment of them will always be fleeting. Only God's daily grace makes us truly grow and thrive.

Ten Percent

*The earth is the LORD's,
and everything in it.*

PSALM 24:1 NLT

Do you tithe? Giving 10 percent of your income specifically to God's work is a good discipline. But sometimes we act as though that 10 percent is God's and the other 90 percent is ours. We forget that *everything* is God's. Through grace, He shares all of creation with us. When we look at it that way, our 10 percent tithe seems a little stingy!

What You Need

Give me neither poverty nor riches!
Give me just enough to
satisfy my needs.

PROVERBS 30:8 NLT

God gives us what we need, and He knows
exactly what and how much that is. Whatever
He has given you financially, He knows that
is what you need right now. Trust His grace.
He will satisfy your needs.

Depth of God's Riches

Oh, the depth of the riches of the wisdom and knowledge of God! How unsearchable his judgments, and his paths beyond tracing out!

ROMANS 11:33 NIV

Money is the way our culture measures value, but we forget that it's just a symbol, a unit of measurement that can never span the infinite value of God's grace. Imagine trying to use a tape measure to stretch across the galaxy, or a teaspoon to determine how much water is in the sea. In the same way, money will always fall short if we use it to try to understand the depth of God's riches.

All You Really Need

Don't wear yourself out trying to get rich; be wise enough to control yourself.

PROVERBS 23:4 NCV

Some nights we lie awake worrying about bills that need to be paid. When Sunday comes, we sit in church preoccupied with how we can afford to pay for a new car, our kids' college bills, or the taxes. We think about the things we would like to buy. And then we work harder and harder to earn the money we think we have to have.

When you catch yourself doing that—stop! God's grace is all you really need.

Others

Sharing Life

*But if we walk in the light,
God himself being the light,
we also experience a shared life
with one another.*

1 JOHN 1:7 MSG

Some of us are extroverts, and some of us
are introverts. But either way, God asks
us to share our lives in some way with
others. As we walk in His light, He gives
us grace to experience a new kind of
a life, a life we have in common with the
others who share His kingdom.

Loving Support

*Let us think of ways to motivate
one another to acts of love
and good works.*

HEBREWS 10:24 NLT

Imagine that you're sitting in the bleachers
watching one of your favorite young people
play a sport. You jump up and cheer for
him. You make sure he knows you're there,
shouting out encouragement. Hearing your
voice, he jumps higher, runs faster.

That is the sort of excitement and
support we need to show others around us.
When we do all we can to encourage
each other, love and good deeds will
burst from us all.

Christ Followers

*"This is what the L*ORD *All-Powerful says:*
'Do what is right and true.
Be kind and merciful to each other.' "

ZECHARIAH 7:9 NCV

As Christ's followers, we need to interact with others the way He did when He was on earth. That means we don't lie to each other, and we don't use others. Instead, we practice kindness and mercy. We let God's grace speak through our mouths.

Overflowing Love

And may the Lord make your love for one another and for all people grow and overflow, just as our love for you overflows.

1 Thessalonians 3:12 NLT

As a very young child, you thought you were the center of the world. As you grew older, you had to go through the painful process of learning that others' feelings were as important as yours. God's grace wants to lift your perspective even higher, though. He wants you to overflow with love for other people.

Past

Healed Past

*"All their past sins will be
forgotten, and they will live
because of the righteous things
they have done."*

Ezekiel 18:22 NLT

We have the feeling that we can't do anything about the past. We think all our mistakes are back there behind us, carved in stone. But God's creative power is amazing, and His grace can heal even the past. Yesterday's sins are pulled out like weeds, while the good things we have done are watered so that they grow and flourish into the present. Give your past to God. His grace is big enough to bring healing even to your worst memories.

Looking Forward

I focus on this one thing:
Forgetting the past and looking
forward to what lies ahead.

PHILIPPIANS 3:13 NLT

As followers of Christ, we are people who look forward rather than backward. We have all made mistakes, but God does not want us to dwell on them, wallowing in guilt and discouragement. Instead, He calls us to let go of the past, trusting Him to deal with it. His grace is new every moment.

Renewal

"Look, the winter is past, and the rains are over and gone."

SONG OF SOLOMON 2:11 NLT

Dreary times of cold and rain come to us all. Just as the earth needs those times to renew itself, so do we. As painful as those times are, grace works through them to make us into the people God has called us to be.

But once those times are over, there's no need to continue to dwell on them. Go outside and enjoy the sunshine!

You Will Live

*Their past sins will be forgiven,
and they will live.*

EZEKIEL 33:16 CEV

Do you ever feel doomed? Do you feel as though your mistakes are waiting to fall on your head, like a huge rock that will crush the life out of you?

We all have moments like that. But God's grace doesn't let that enormous boulder drop. His forgiveness catches it and rolls it away. You will live after all!

Patience

Valuable

Better to be patient than powerful; better to have self-control than to conquer a city.

PROVERBS 16:32 NLT

Our world values visible power. We appreciate things like prestige and skill, wealth and influence. But God looks at things differently. From His perspective, the quiet, easily overlooked quality of patience is far more valuable than any worldly power. Patience makes room for others' needs and brokenness. Patience creates a space in our lives for God's grace to flow through us.

Quiet Time

Be still before the LORD,
and wait patiently for him.

PSALM 37:7 NRSV

Our lives are busy. Responsibilities crowd our days, and at night as we go to bed, our minds often continue to be preoccupied with the day's work, ticking off a mental to-do list even as we fall asleep.

We need to set aside time to quiet our hearts. In those moments, we can let go of all our to-dos and wait for God's grace to take action in our lives.

Quiet Grace

Patient persistence pierces through indifference; gentle speech breaks down rigid defenses.

PROVERBS 25:15 MSG

When we're in the midst of an argument, we often become fixated on winning. We turn conflicts into power struggles, and we want to come out the victor. By sheer force, if necessary, we want to shape people to our will.

But that is not the way God treats us. His grace is gentle and patient rather than loud and forceful. We need to follow His example and let His quiet grace speak through us in His timing rather than ours.

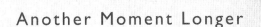

Another Moment Longer

Wait patiently for the LORD.
Be brave and courageous.
Yes, wait patiently for the LORD.

PSALM 27:14 NLT

Patience is all about waiting things out. It's about holding on another moment longer. It means enduring hard times. As a younger person, you probably felt you couldn't possibly endure certain things, but the older you get, the more you realize that you can. If you just wait long enough, the tide always turns. Hold on. Your life will change. God's grace will rescue you.

Peace

Peaceful Hearts

*You will keep in perfect
peace all who trust in you,
all whose thoughts are fixed on you!*

ISAIAH 26:3 NLT

Peace seems very far away sometimes. But it's not! Peace isn't an emotion we can work up in our own strength. It's one of the gifts of grace God longs to give us. All we need to do is focus on Him. As we give Him all our worries, one by one, every day, He will do His part: He will keep our hearts at peace.

Peace Rules

*And let the peace that comes
from Christ rule in your hearts.
For as members of one body you
are called to live in peace.*

COLOSSIANS 3:15 NLT

Peace is a way of living our lives. It happens
when we let Christ's peace into our lives to
rule over our emotions, our doubts, and our
worries, and then go one step more and let
His peace control the way we live. Peace is
God's gift of grace to us, but it is also the way
to a graceful life, the path to harmony
with the world around us.

Prayer

An All-the-Time Thing!

*Pray diligently. Stay alert,
with your eyes wide open
in gratitude.*

COLOSSIANS 4:2 MSG

Prayer is not a sometimes thing. It's an all-the-time thing! We need to pray every day, being careful to keep the lines of communication open between God and ourselves all through the day, moment by moment. When we make prayer a habit, we won't miss the many gifts of grace that come our way. And we won't forget to notice when God answers our prayers.

The Center of Our Lives

The apostles often met together and prayed with a single purpose in mind.

ACTS 1:14 CEV

What do you do when you get together with the people you're close to? You probably talk and laugh, share a meal, maybe go shopping or work on a project. But do you ever pray together?

If prayer is the center of our lives, we will want to share this gift of grace with those with whom we're closest.

Alone Time
with God

*But Jesus often withdrew
to the wilderness for prayer.*

LUKE 5:16 NLT

God is always with us, even when we're too busy to do more than whisper a prayer in the shower or as we drive the car. But if even Jesus needed to make time to get away by Himself for some alone time with God, then we certainly need to do so, too.

In those quiet moments of prayer, by ourselves with God, we will find the grace we need to live our busy lives.

He's Waiting. . .

"The eyes of the Lord watch over those who do right, and his ears are open to their prayers."

1 PETER 3:12 NLT

You don't have to try to get God's attention. He is watching you right now. His ear is tuned to your voice. All you need to do is speak, and He will hear you. Receive the gift of grace He gives to you through prayer. Tell God your thoughts, your feelings, your hopes, your joys. He's waiting to listen to you.

Present

Right Now

*For God says, "At just the right time,
I heard you. On the day of salvation,
I helped you." Indeed, the "right time"
is now. Today is the day of salvation.*

2 CORINTHIANS 6:2 NLT

God always meets us right now, in the present moment. We don't need to waste our time looking over our shoulders at the past, and we don't have to feel as though we need to reach some future moment before we can truly touch God. He is here now. Today, this very moment, is full of His grace.

See Jesus

God left nothing that is not subject to him. Yet at present we do not see everything subject to him. But we see Jesus.

HEBREWS 2:8–9 NIV

We know that Jesus has won the victory over sin, and yet when we look at the world as it is right now, we still see sin all around us. We see pain and suffering, greed and selfishness, brokenness and despair. We know that the world is not ruled by God. Yet despite that, we can look past the darkness of sin. By grace, right now, we can see Jesus.

Constant Grace

For Jesus doesn't change—
yesterday, today, tomorrow,
he's always totally himself.

HEBREWS 13:8 MSG

As human beings, we live in the stream of time. Sometimes all the changes time brings terrify us; sometimes they fill us with joy and excitement. Either way, we can cling to the still point that lies in the middle of our changing world: Jesus Christ, who never changes. His constant grace leads us through all life's changes, and one day it will bring us to our home in heaven, beyond time, where we will be like Him.

The Present Moment

"This day is sacred to our Lord."
NEHEMIAH 8:10 NIV

Sometimes we're in such a hurry to get to the future that we miss out on the present. God has gifts He wants to give you right now. Don't be so excited about tomorrow that you overlook the grace He's giving you today.

Today's Opportunities

But encourage each other every day while it is "today." Help each other so none of you will become hardened because sin has tricked you.

HEBREWS 3:13 NCV

Don't put off helping others. Sin tricks us into thinking we can do it later. But grace doesn't procrastinate. Take advantage of the opportunities that come your way today.

Quiet

A Quiet Pace

"Teach me, and I will be quiet.
Show me where I have been wrong."

JOB 6:24 NCV

Do you ever feel as though you simply can't sit still? That your thoughts are swirling so fast that you can't stop them? That you're so busy, so stressed, so hurried that you have to run, run, run?

Take a breath. Open your heart to God. Allow Him to quiet your frantic mind. Ask Him to show you how you can begin again, this time walking to the quiet pace of His grace.

Relax. . .

But I am calm and quiet,
like a baby with its mother.
I am at peace, like a baby
with its mother.

PSALM 131:2 NCV

You know how a baby lies completely limp in her mother's arms, totally trusting and at peace? That is the attitude you need to practice. Let yourself relax in God's arms, wrapped in His grace. Life will go on around you, with all its noise and turmoil. Meanwhile, you are completely safe, totally secure, without a worry in the world. Lie back and enjoy the quiet!

New Strength

*"In quietness and confidence
is your strength."*

ISAIAH 30:15 NLT

The weaker we feel, the more we fret.
The more we fret, the weaker we feel. It's
a vicious circle.

Stop the circle! Find a quiet place, if
only for a few moments, to draw close to
God. Grace will come to you through the
quiet, and you will discover new strength.

Near at Hand

*Quiet down before GOD,
be prayerful before him.*

PSALM 37:7 MSG

It's not easy to be quiet. Our world is loud, and the noise seeps into our hearts and minds. We feel restless and jumpy, on edge. God seems far away.

But God is always near at hand, no matter how we feel. When we quiet our hearts, we will find Him there, patiently waiting, ready to show us His grace.

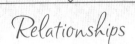

Relationships

Because of Christ

*All this comes from the God who
settled the relationship between us
and him, and then called us to settle
our relationships with each other.*

2 CORINTHIANS 5:18 MSG

God created a bridge to span the
distance between ourselves and Him.
That bridge is Christ, the best and fullest
expression of divine grace. Because of
Christ, we are in a relationship with
the Creator of the entire world. And
because of Christ, we are called to
build bridges of our own, to span the
distance between ourselves and others.

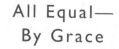

All Equal—
By Grace

Live in peace with each other.
Do not be proud, but make friends
with those who seem unimportant.
Do not think how smart you are.

Sometimes other people just seem so stupid! We pride ourselves that *we* would never act like that, dress like that, talk like that. But God wants us to let go of our pride. He wants us to remember that in His eyes we are all equal, all loved, all saved only by grace.

Only by Grace

Accept one another, then,
just as Christ accepted you,
in order to bring praise to God.

ROMANS 15:7 NIV

It's easy to pick out others' faults. Sometimes you may even feel justified in doing so, as though God will approve of your righteousness as you point out others' sinfulness.

Don't forget that Christ accepted you, with all your brokenness and faults. Only by grace were you made whole. Share that grace—that acceptance and unconditional love—with the people around you.

Simply Love

But I am giving you a new command.
You must love each other,
just as I have loved you.

JOHN 13:34 CEV

Christ doesn't ask us to point out others' faults. He doesn't require that we be the morality squad, focusing on all that is sinful in the world around us. Instead, He wants us to simply love, just as He loves us. When we do, the world will see God's grace shining in our lives.

Renewal

From the Inside Out

*Take on an entirely new way of life—
a God-fashioned life, a life renewed
from the inside and working itself
into your conduct as God accurately
reproduces his character in you.*

EPHESIANS 4:24 MSG

At the end of a long week, we sometimes
feel tired and drained. We need to
use feelings like that as wake-up calls,
reminders that we need to open ourselves anew to God's Spirit so that He
can renew us from the inside out.
Grace has the power to change our
hearts and minds, filling us with new
energy to follow Jesus.

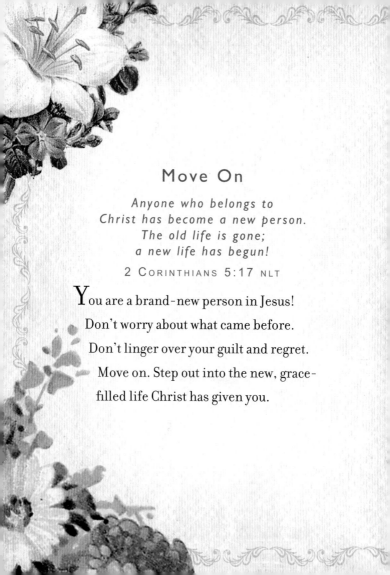

Move On

*Anyone who belongs to
Christ has become a new person.
The old life is gone;
a new life has begun!*

2 CORINTHIANS 5:17 NLT

You are a brand-new person in Jesus!
Don't worry about what came before.
Don't linger over your guilt and regret.
Move on. Step out into the new, grace-
filled life Christ has given you.

Fresh Hearts

*"I will give you a new heart
and put a new spirit within you."*

EZEKIEL 36:26 NKJV

Life is full of irritations and hassles. Bills to pay, errands to run, arguments to settle, and endless responsibilities all stress our hearts until we feel old and worn.

But God renews us. Day after day, over and over, His grace comes to us, making our hearts fresh and green and growing.

Drawing Back the Curtains

But whenever someone turns to the Lord, the veil is taken away. . . . So all of us who have had that veil removed can see and reflect the glory of the Lord. And the Lord— who is the Spirit—makes us more and more like him as we are changed into his glorious image.

2 CORINTHIANS 3:16, 18 NLT

Sometime we feel as though a thick dark curtain hangs between us and God, hiding Him from our sight. But the Bible says that all we have to do is turn our hearts to the Lord and the curtain will be drawn back, letting God's glory and grace shine into our lives. When that happens, we can soak up the light, allowing it to renew our hearts and minds into the image of Christ.

Rest

Take a Break

"Only in returning to me and resting in me will you be saved."

ISAIAH 30:15 NLT

Some days you try everything you can think of to save yourself, but no matter how hard you try, you fail again and again. You fall on your face and embarrass yourself. You hurt the people around you. You make mistakes, and nothing whatsoever seems to go right.

When that happens, it's time to take a break. You need to stop trying so hard. Throw yourself in God's arms. Rest on His grace, knowing that He will save you.

Quiet, Gentle Grace

"Let me teach you, because I am humble and gentle at heart, and you will find rest for your souls."

MATTHEW 11:29 NLT

Sometimes we keep trying to do things on our own, even though we don't know what we're doing and even though we're exhausted. And all the while, Jesus waits quietly, ready to show us the way. He will lead us with quiet, gentle grace, carrying our burdens for us. We don't have to try so hard. We can finally rest.

Sleep in Peace

*At day's end I'm ready
for sound sleep,
For you, God, have put my
life back together.*

PSALM 4:8 MSG

At the end of the day, let everything—
good and bad together—drop into God's
hands. You can sleep in peace, knowing
that meanwhile God will continue to work,
healing all that is broken in your life. Relax
in His grace.

Mind, Body, Spirit. . .

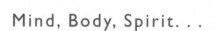

*I stretch myself out. I sleep.
Then I'm up again—rested,
tall and steady.*

PSALM 3:5 MSG

Rest is one of God's gifts to us, a gift we regularly need. In sleep, we are renewed, mind, body, and spirit. Don't turn away from this most natural and practical of gifts!

Solitude

Welcome Interruptions

*So they left by boat for a quiet place,
where they could be alone.*

MARK 6:32 NLT

Jesus and the disciples sought a quiet
place, away from the crowds. Like us,
they needed alone time. But as so often
happens, people interrupt those moments
of solitude. The crowd follows us, the phone
rings, someone comes to the door.
When that happens, we must ask Jesus
for the grace to follow His example
and let go of our quiet moments
alone, welcoming the interruption with
patience and love.

Always Present

*Lord, you have been watching.
Do not keep quiet. Lord,
do not leave me alone.*

PSALM 35:22 NCV

Have you ever seen a child suddenly look up from playing, realize she's all alone, and then run to get her mother's attention? Meanwhile, her mother was watching her all along.

Sometimes solitude is a good thing— and other times, it's just plain lonely.

When loneliness turns into isolation, remember that God's loving eyes are always on you. He will never leave you all alone, and His grace is always present.

All Alone

"But when you pray, go away
by yourself, shut the door behind you,
and pray to your Father in private.
Then your Father, who sees everything,
will reward you."

MATTHEW 6:6 NLT

Prayer takes many shapes and forms.
There's the corporate kind of prayer, in
which we open our hearts to God as part of
a congregation. There is also the kind of
prayer that is said quickly and on the run.
But we need to make at least some time in
our lives for the prayer in the privacy of
some quiet place, when we meet
God's grace all alone.

The Right People

*The LORD God said, "It isn't good for the
man to live alone. I need to make
a suitable partner for him."*

GENESIS 2:18 CEV

God understands that human beings need
each other. His love comes to us through
others. That is the way He designed us, and
we can trust His grace to bring the right
people along when we need them, the people
who will banish our loneliness and share our
lives.

Strength

Praise Him!

*The Lord is my strength, my song,
and my salvation. He is my God,
and I will praise him.*

EXODUS 15:2 TLB

God makes you strong; He makes you sing with gladness; and He rescues you from sin. These are the gifts of His grace.

When He has given you so much, don't you want to give back to Him? Use your strength, your joy, and your freedom to praise Him.

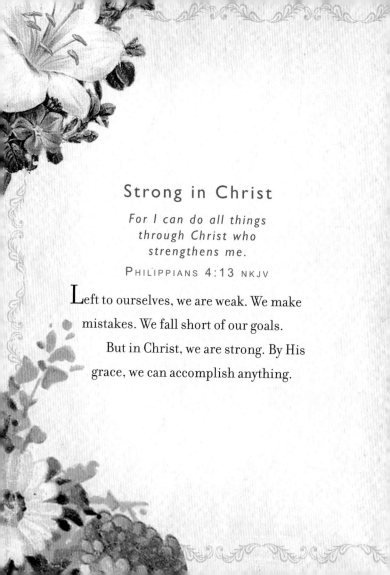

Strong in Christ

*For I can do all things
through Christ who
strengthens me.*

PHILIPPIANS 4:13 NKJV

Left to ourselves, we are weak. We make
mistakes. We fall short of our goals.

But in Christ, we are strong. By His
grace, we can accomplish anything.

Today—
and Tomorrow

You are my strong shield, and I trust you completely. You have helped me, and I will celebrate and thank you in song.

PSALM 28:7 CEV

God proves Himself to us over and over again. And yet over and over, we doubt His power. We need to learn from experience. The God whose strength rescued us yesterday and the day before will certainly rescue us again today. As we celebrate the grace we received yesterday and the day before, we gain confidence and faith for today and tomorrow.

Lifted Up

*But those who trust in the
LORD will find new strength.
They will soar high on wings like eagles.
They will run and not grow weary.
They will walk and not faint.*

ISAIAH 40:31 NLT

Do you ever have days when you ask
yourself, "How much further can I go? How
much longer can I keep going like this?" On
days like that, you long to give up. You wish
you could just run away from the world and
hide.

Trust God's grace to give you the
strength you need, even then. Let Him lift
you up on eagle's wings.

Success

Where Credit Is Due

*It is not that we think we are
qualified to do anything on our own.
Our qualification comes from God.*

2 CORINTHIANS 3:5 NLT

It's easy to seek God when we feel like
failures, but when success comes our way,
we like to congratulate ourselves rather
than give God the credit. When we achieve
great things, we need to remember
that it is God's grace through us that
brought about our success.

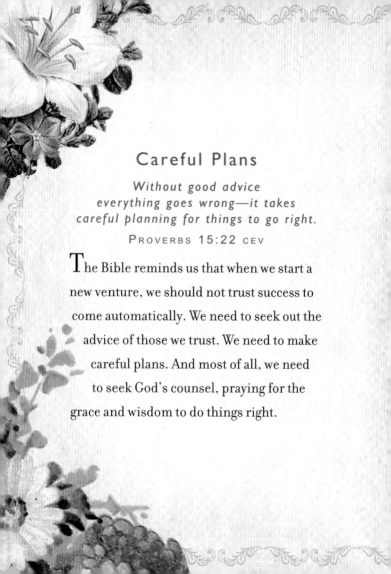

Careful Plans

*Without good advice
everything goes wrong—it takes
careful planning for things to go right.*

PROVERBS 15:22 CEV

The Bible reminds us that when we start a new venture, we should not trust success to come automatically. We need to seek out the advice of those we trust. We need to make careful plans. And most of all, we need to seek God's counsel, praying for the grace and wisdom to do things right.

Wonderful!

*Commit your actions to the LORD,
and your plans will succeed.*

PROVERBS 16:3 NLT

Just because we *want* something to happen,
doesn't mean it will, no matter how hard
we pray. We've all found that out (often to
our sorrow!). But when we truly commit
everything we do to God, praying only for
His grace to be given free rein in our lives,
then we will be surprised by what comes
about. It may not be what we imagined—
but it will be wonderful!

Whatever Comes Next

"You will succeed in whatever you choose to do, and light will shine on the road ahead of you."

JOB 22:28 NLT

The word *success* originally meant simply "the thing that comes next." Over the years, we've added to that meaning the sense that success has to be the thing we wanted to happen, the outcome for which we hoped.

But God does not necessarily define success the way we do. Whatever comes next, no matter what, His grace transforms it, using circumstances to create the light we need to travel still further on our road to heaven.

Talents

Vehicle for God's Grace

Do not neglect your gift. . . .
Be diligent in these matters;
give yourself wholly to them, so that
everyone may see your progress.

1 TIMOTHY 4:14–15 NIV

God expects us to use the talents He gave us. Don't turn away from them with a false sense of modesty. Exercise them. Improve your skills. Whatever your gift may be, use it as a vehicle for God's grace.

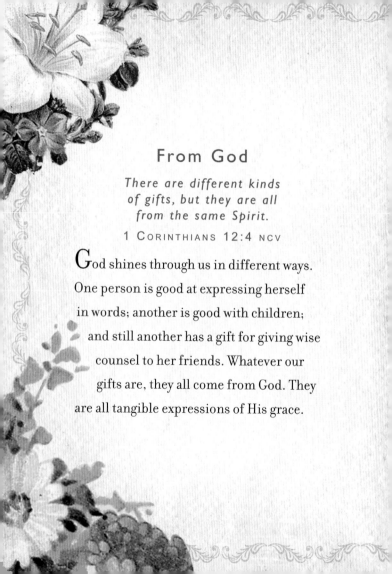

From God

*There are different kinds
of gifts, but they are all
from the same Spirit.*

1 CORINTHIANS 12:4 NCV

God shines through us in different ways.
One person is good at expressing herself
in words; another is good with children;
and still another has a gift for giving wise
counsel to her friends. Whatever our
gifts are, they all come from God. They
are all tangible expressions of His grace.

Use Your Gift

Each of you has been blessed with one of God's many wonderful gifts to be used in the service of others. So use your gift well.

1 PETER 4:10 CEV

God did not give you your talents for your own pleasure only. These skills you have were meant to be offered to the world. He wants to use them to build His kingdom here on earth.

So pick up your skill, whatever it is, and use it to bring grace to someone's life.

Creative Expression

Not only has the LORD filled him with his Spirit, but he has given him wisdom and made him a skilled craftsman who can create objects of art with gold, silver, bronze, stone, and wood.

EXODUS 35:31 CEV

We were designed to be creative people. Whether we sew clothes or paint pictures, come up with new business ideas or write stories, make a welcoming home or cook delicious meals, God's creativity longs to be expressed through us. As we exercise our creative talents, we are united with Him. His Spirit works through our hands, creating visions of grace as we make the world a lovelier place for us all.

Time

Outside of Time's Stream

*Your throne, O LORD, has stood from
time immemorial. You yourself are
from the everlasting past.*

PSALM 93:2 NLT

If you think of time as a fast-moving river,
then we are creatures caught in its stream.
Life keeps slipping away from us like water
between our fingers.

But God is outside of time's stream. He
holds our past safely in His hands, and
His grace is permanent and unshakable.
His love is the lifesaver to which we cling
in the midst of time's wild waves.

Meant to Move

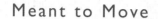

*We are only foreigners living
here on earth for a while,
just as our ancestors were.
And we will soon be gone, like a
shadow that suddenly disappears.*

1 CHRONICLES 29:15 CEV

We are not meant to feel too at home
in this world. Maybe that is why time is
designed to keep us from lingering too long
in one place. We are meant to be moving
on, making our way to our forever-home
in heaven. Grace has brought us safe
thus far—and grace will lead us home.

Young

*Honor and enjoy your Creator
while you're still young.*

ECCLESIASTES 12:1 MSG

Young is a matter of perspective. Some people are old at fifteen, and others are still young at ninety. As we enjoy the God who made us, honoring Him in all we do, His grace will keep us young.

Sense of Timing

But do not forget this one thing,
dear friends: With the Lord a day
is like a thousand years, and a
thousand years are like a day.

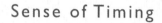

2 PETER 3:8 NIV

God's sense of timing is not the same
as ours. What seems like forever to us, an
impossible time to wait for something, God
sees as exactly the right amount of time,
a mere blink of the eye. And on the other
hand, God's grace can use a split second to
change a person's life.

Truth

Adorned with Grace

*Don't ever forget kindness and truth.
Wear them like a necklace.*

PROVERBS 3:3 NCV

Kindness and truth are strands of the same necklace. You should not be so kind that you evade the truth, nor should you be so truthful that you wound others. Instead, adorn yourselves with both strands of this necklace. Wear it with grace.

What's Real

*"Then you will experience
for yourselves the truth,
and the truth will free you."*

JOHN 8:32 MSG

Truth is what is real, while lies are nothing but words. God wants us to experience what is truly real. Sometimes we would rather hide from reality, but grace comes to us through truth. No matter how painful the truth may sometimes seem, it will ultimately set us free.

On Truth's Side

We're rooting for the truth to win out in you. We couldn't possibly do otherwise.

2 CORINTHIANS 13:8 MSG

As we look at the world around us, we can see that people often prefer falsehoods to truth. They choose to live in a world that soothes their anxiety, rather than face life's reality. We cannot force people to acknowledge what they don't want to face, but we can do all we can to encourage them and build them up. We can cheer for the truth, trusting that God's grace is always on truth's side.

True Essence

"God is spirit, and those who worship him must worship in spirit and truth."

JOHN 4:24 NCV

We might be able to fool the flesh-and-blood people around us, but we cannot deceive the Spirit of God. He sees our truest essence. The only way to come into His presence is to accept our own truth—and offer it up to Him. May He give us the grace to truly worship Him!

Understanding

The Missing Pieces

Trust the Lord with all your heart, and don't depend on your own understanding.

PROVERBS 3:5 NCV

Life is confusing. No matter how hard we try, we can't always make sense of it. We don't like it when that happens, and so we keep trying to determine what's going on, as though we were trying puzzle pieces to fill in a picture we long to see. Sometimes, though, we have to accept that in this life we will never be able to see the entire image. We have to trust God's grace for the missing pieces.

Growing in Grace

This is my prayer for you:
that your love will grow more
and more; that you will have
knowledge and understanding
with your love.

PHILIPPIANS 1:9 NCV

God wants us to be spiritually mature. He
wants us to love more deeply, and at the
same time, He wants us to reach deeper
into wisdom and understanding. This is
not something we can accomplish in our
own strength with our own abilities. Only
God can make us grow in grace.

Most Important

Tune your ears to the world of Wisdom; set your heart on a life of Understanding.

PROVERBS 2:3 MSG

What do you listen to most? Do you hear the world's voice, telling you to buy, buy, buy; to dress and look a certain way; to focus on things that won't last? Or have you tuned your ears to hear the quiet voice of God's wisdom? You can tell the answer to that question by your response to yet another question: What is most important to you? Things? Or the intangible grace of true understanding?

Walking with Grace

"Give me an understanding heart so that I can govern your people well and know the difference between right and wrong."

1 KINGS 3:9 NLT

We are not kings who rule nations, but all of us have spheres of influence and authority, whether at home or at work. As Christ's followers, we must be careful not to abuse our authority. Instead, we should seek to understand, to walk with grace the straight path of kindness and wisdom.

Wealth

First Priorities

For Wisdom is better than all the trappings of wealth; nothing you could wish for holds a candle to her.

PROVERBS 8:11 MSG

What do you value most? You may know the answer you are "supposed" to give to that question, but you can tell the real answer by where your time and energy are focused. Do you spend most of your time working for and thinking about money and physical wealth, or do you make wisdom and grace your first priorities?

Grace Multiplied

*Honor the LORD with your
wealth and with the best part
of everything you produce.*

PROVERBS 3:9 NLT

We connect the word *wealth* with money,
but long ago the word meant "happiness,
prosperity, well-being." If you think about
your wealth in this light, then the word
encompasses far more of your life. Your
health, your abilities, your friends, your
family, your physical strength, and your
creative energy—all of these are parts
of your true wealth. Grace brought all of
these riches into your life, and when we use
them to honor God, grace is multiplied
still more.

Never Bought

They trust in their riches and
brag about all of their wealth.
You cannot buy back your
life or pay off God!

PSALM 49:6–7 CEV

We humans are easily confused about what real wealth is. We think that money can make us strong. We assume that physical possessions will enhance our importance and dignity in others' eyes.

But life is not for sale. And grace can never be bought.

Riches That Last

"Yes, a person is a fool to store up earthly wealth but not have a rich relationship with God."

LUKE 12:21 NLT

W hy would we want money in the bank and a house full of stuff if we lived in a world that was empty of grace? Only in God do we find the riches that will last forever.

Wisdom

Wise Enough to Lead

*"To God belong wisdom and power;
counsel and understanding are his."*

JOB 12:13 NIV

The word *wisdom* comes from the same
root words that have to do with vision,
the ability to see into a deeper spiritual
reality. Where else can we turn for the grace
to see beneath life's surface except to
God? Who else can we trust to be strong
enough and wise enough to lead us to
our eternal home?

Building God's Kingdom

*And I have filled him with the Spirit
of God, in wisdom and ability,
in understanding and intelligence,
and in knowledge, and in all
kinds of craftsmanship.*

EXODUS 31:3 AMP

Your abilities, your intelligence, your
knowledge, and your talents are all gifts
of grace from God's generous Spirit. But
without wisdom, the ability to see into
the spiritual world, none of these gifts
is worth very much. Wisdom is what fits
together all of the other pieces, allowing us
to use our talents to build God's spiritual
kingdom.

Nothing More
Valuable

Wisdom is more valuable than gold and crystal. It cannot be purchased with jewels mounted in fine gold.

JOB 28:17 NLT

Money can't buy you love—and it can't buy wisdom either. Wisdom is more precious than anything this world has to offer. In fact, some passages of the Old Testament seem to indicate that Wisdom is another name for Jesus. Just as Jesus is the Way, the Truth, and the Life, He is also the One who gives us the vision to see God's world all around us. No other gift is more valuable than Jesus.

Secret Places

*Yet, you desire truth and sincerity.
Deep down inside me
you teach me wisdom.*

PSALM 51:6 GWT

Sometimes we are like Adam and Eve in the garden after they had sinned; we are afraid to come naked into God's presence. We think we can hide ourselves from Him. But God cannot teach our hearts if we refuse to be open with Him. We must take the risk of stepping into His presence with complete honesty and vulnerability. When we do, His grace touches us at our deepest, most secret places, and we are filled with His wisdom.

Work

Control

*Put GOD in charge of your work,
then what you've planned
will take place*

PROVERBS 16:3 MSG

If we're doing a job that is important to us,
it is hard to let go of our control. Not only
do we hate to trust someone else to take
over, but we often don't want to trust God
to take charge either. We want to do it
all by ourselves. But the best laid plans
fall into nothing without God's help.
What's more, as we rely on His grace,
we no longer need to feel stressed or
pressured! We can let Him take charge.

Heaven's Perspective

*Always give yourselves
fully to the work of the Lord,
because you know that your labor
in the Lord is not in vain.*

1 CORINTHIANS 15:58 NIV

You may feel sometimes as though all of your hard work comes to nothing. But if your work is the Lord's work, you can trust Him to bring it to fulfillment. You may not always know what is being accomplished in the light of eternity, but God knows. And when you look back from heaven's perspective, you will be able to see how much grace was accomplished through all of your hard work.

The Bigger
Picture

*"But you, be strong and do not lose
courage, for there is reward
for your work."*

2 CHRONICLES 15:7 NASB

Why do you work? For a paycheck? For
respect? For a sense of self-worth? All
of those things are good reasons to work,
but never forget that your work is part of a
bigger picture. God wants to use your hands,
your intelligence, and your efforts to build
His kingdom, the place where grace
dwells.

Old Testament

Proverbs

New Testament

Philippians

Colossians

1 Thessalonians

2 Thessalonians

1 Timothy

2 Timothy

Notes

Notes

Notes

Notes

Notes

Notes

Notes